Changelings
&
Omen Birds

Poems by Claire Clube

RAILROAD STREET PRESS

Copyright © 2017

All rights reserved

Printed in the United States of America

LIBRARY OF CONGRESS
CATALOGING-IN-PUBLICATION DATA

Clube, Claire
Changelings & Omen Birds / Claire Clube

ISBN 9781936711437

10 9 8 7 6 5 4 3 2 1

Railroad Street Press
394 Railroad St., Ste 2
St. Johnsbury, VT 05819

Copyright © 2017 Jake Rosenzweig
By Inheritance
Claire Clube Rosenzweig, 1964-2013

To Jake and Bess

- from your Mother
2011

Acknowledgments: Poet Larry Bradley, Second Reader, NEVERMORE Bookstore, Newport, VT; Nikita Lalwani, Boston Globe Correspondent; Denise Piette, Copy & Cover Design at The Front Desk, Newport, VT; Diane Peel, Media Connection at The 99 Art Gallery, Newport, VT; Jeanne Pray, Agency & Finance at Passumpsic Bank, Newport, VT; Cover Photograph- amazinglytimedphotos.com; Back Cover Photograph Courtesy Of Caley Beard; Title Page Illustration By Elihu Vedder; Sketch From The Rubiyat, Author's Collection; End Papers Illustration; Thumbeblina: May Queen, From The Collection Of Tom Farrow.

This Edition Is Dedicated To Mr. & Mrs. Jacob Rosenzweig, Malcolm Clube, Diana Mathews-Duncan, Liam Rector & The Bennington MFA Class Of January 2008.

Also By Claire Clube:

Dora & Other Poems. Privately Printed By The Author
2008.

RAPT ROCKS: Poetry, Photography & Design
By The Author
The British Museum, 2003

The Comstock Review;
Award of Special Merit
Fall 2010/Winter 2011

Contents

Damson Longing

2	And Something
3	Peppermint Fence
4	Weights and Measures
5	Almost and the Art of It
6	Mimicry
8	Milk Clouds and Damson-Longing

Work

10	Scry
11	Bruise
12	Guitar
13	Selkie
14	Begotten
15	The Moon Reveals Her Shadow
16	Advent
17	The Fish
18	Knot
19	Intersection
20	Live Haulage
21	Vole
22	Work

Made by Hand

24	Dear Mr Ammons
27	Aurelia Aurata
28	Wake
29	Roadkill

30	Filament
31	Claiggan Bay, Islay
32	Finding the Semibreve
33	Offering
34	Made by Hand
35	Notes
36	Germination
37	Prayer
38	Mordant
40	Listen
41	Seal
42	Tincture
43	Do I Qualify
44	Words Like Skylarks
45	Finding Mu
46	When the Soul Wakes
47	I'm Not a Lover of Love Poems
48	These Are How Delicate?
50	Room 6 1 2

Drawing with the Heart's Line

52	Elemental
53	Translation
54	Dorset/Peru, Vermont
55	Dora
56	Blue Milk
58	Infusion
59	Annunciation
60	Blue
61	Loon
62	Inscription
63	How Long Have You Been Satisfied?

64   Cave Valley, Zion
65   Life Cycle
67   Tumbleweed
68   Asteroid 433
69   Flutter

The Consequences of Intimacy

71   The Boyle's King
72   Collide
73   Skin
74   All That's Possible
75   Femur
77   Renegade
78   Bird
79   Talking to Myself
80   Words of the Night-Time Angels

Gone to Earth

82   Black and Blue
83   Gull
86   megapera novaeangliae, the big wings of the sea
89   An Autobiographical Sequence Poem Taken from the Story of Thumbelina
89   Light Found in the Boom of Things.
90   Indigo Child.
91   Self Portrait.

Preface By Sean Andrew Heaney

In 2013, I had the honor of reading the final draft of Claire's exquisite manuscript, "CHANGELINGS & OMEN BIRDS." Would that she had the gifts of prophecy and foreknowledge that would have prevented her from leaving England on what tragically proved to be a one way passage.

She was leaving for another trip to Africa with her daughter, Bess. She intended to look at properties there so she could divide residency between Capetown, South Africa and a seaside cottage in Scotland. She was a naturalist by her very nature, who was most in her element in the wild, exploring new landscapes, and as a traveler, truly a bird on the wing. She had fallen in love with Africa, and her daughter was a Georgetown graduate, who specialized in African studies and languages. They meant to teach Arts Education to young children as part of The Lalela Project, that brings the Arts to many towns and villages.

Claire had earned her Master's in Poetry, her abiding love, in the esteemed Bennington MFA Program, but in truth she was a Master of ALL Fine Arts. She was a sculptor, clothes designer, jewelry maker, self taught designer of limited edition books as *objet d'arts*, a painter, weaver and superb photographer.

She was fiercely devoted to her son and daughter, following Jake's auto racing career in person, and often having Bess as her travelling companion on other journeys. I had received many calls from Claire-in-Transit, telling me her estimated times of arrival and departure. She was strong when she had to be, a truly devoted friend and the most generous soul I have ever known.

She was a delicate, finely tuned instrument whose keen vision saw the world in macrocosm, microcosm and the world in front of her with crystal clarity. To be attuned to the natural world and one's own nature makes for a rare spirit: to be able to capture that on the page makes a poet.

On July 25th, 2013, the woman who wanted wings and her fledgling beauty were lost when their plane from Kenya crashed in Aberdere National Park. The cause of the accident remains a mystery.

The search and rescue effort took three days to find the crash site and recover the bodies of the pilot and his two passengers. The search party was greeted by an unusual sight; a herd of elephants had surrounded the plane as if on vigil. As the team cautiously approached, the elephants turned and slowly filed away. I have no doubt Claire and Bess appreciated this ceremonial blessing of their Rite of Passage to becoming part of everything in heaven and earth. For those of us who remain in the realm, the world is turning a little bit slower from here on out.

This volume contains all the poems of the final draft of "CHANGELINGS & OMEN BIRDS," left by Claire for me to proof read. We both graduated from the Bennington MFA program, Class of January, 2008, so some of her poetry was familiar to me. It was her wish to add a final section to her manuscript ominously titled, GONE TO EARTH. She intended to put her house and her work in order upon her return. She had left behind a turbulent domestic situation, and I found the poetry to be dark waters; the unfinished serial poem for Bess, the Thumbelina Autobiography, was more of an adult fable, with Adult Content throughout. Luckily, she had the final say on her poetry and I was honored that her mother and her son petitioned me to bring her poems into the light.

DAMSON LONGING

And Something

Always strikes.
She never believed them.

There's no time for faithlessness.

So she left before the full moon,
to the dark and such and such

when no one was looking
There's no end to things,

especially silence.

Peppermint Fence

Early evening. Thorn-less.
The wind sculpts
afterglow.

She lies on her back sheltered in dreams,
a betrothal of sorts.

She wants for wings.

We pretend in mute gestures
we know what we're doing.

She presses the promise to her breast.
Petals like a kingfisher's flame

fall through fire.

Weights and Measures

Try and measure ounces with a piece of string.

Make something opaque, transparent.
Make indelible marks to carry with you into the next life.

Leave a trace.

Watch how evening light is made. Who chose the colour
for ghost crabs, measured their violet pink?

Who imprinted the dragon in the evening sky
when you were too busy cramming your feral
eyes with what you couldn't name?

Love is the duplicate. It has no weight.

Measure every gram of loss by letting it go.

Almost and the Art of It

Vanity distorts intimacy.
Take away the safety net.

At night, the moon opens
the lily's mouth, prepares
her gaping skirts for the sun.

This is the day of our daily bread.
This is the day of the windflower,

sundew, barnacle fixed to stone.
We leap to our survival.

Mimicry

Animals dig down, fashioned from instinct.
Little things feel
and shoot
their nodules
heavenwards.

The raven, honed,
divides the light,

a polished wing.

A butterfly drowns in ink.

    *

You like to me, smiling,

cast your aspersions, render me
a ghost child,
with only an outline for a life.

I filled it in.

Swallows score the sky, trailing
pin-thin shadows.

Mother, when will you speak to me?
When will you devour
your own perfection?

Today, poppies,
hollow-coloured in the sun,
open, a tympanum,

a third eye.

Milk Clouds and Damson-Longing

Woman, take off your shell.
Unravel,

wholly appropriate, like seeds curling
out of hard bodies.

Gather your wedding water.

Repeat the refrain,

Lalayeh, oh mi lar, menan ah lamisi.
Lalayeh, oh mi lar, menan ah lamisi.

WORK

Scry
to cry out or divine visions from the natural world's elements and fragments

The raven is slightly soft, thawing
in my room,
the sheen
of his eyes not yet smeared,
wings like fishhooks,

grey inside black, night
meeting morning,
a beak to pierce the world.

Today, I will cut the raven's claws, wings, his head,
leave his body a gourd.

    *

                I will speak
every pivot and dip of my thousand cries,
put on his wings,
       his severed wings.

wing tips that bend to the earth and the sun,

the voice from my heart
a spring from its source.

I will rehearse sounds in the dark,
mimic his body that gapes

to warmth.

Bruise

Street lamps dowse in the dark,
shadows like shale.
A siren calls.
                      Torch red
inside the shafts of my body.
First quarter of the moon.
This day a cut out — a paper
lantern. What did I learn?
No two winds feel the same.
I am filled with purple –
violet seeping black-blue.
That I repair.

Guitar

I store my unspoken words inside
the guitar
frets like laces
securing them tightly.

I remember not to slouch
but to sit comfortably,
clasp the instrument
to my chest,

my fretting hand
poised above the strings.
Opening its throat, sound
expands as if from soft tissue,

clutching the knots inside my body,
cauterizing them, plucking
me from the gallows.
I know nothing now,

driving crotchets, minims,
into extinction, the flotsam
in my head jettisoned
as snow falls,

tapping its stars
against my window,
drowning out the noise
like electrocution.

Selkie

I will be always looking into the sea.

I stand chest deep in water,
level with gulls, grebes, eiders, fishing on the fly.
Two mating crabs with glossy black claws cling to the strings
of my scallop net, spying on me with the tips
of their roller ball eyes.

How am I to inhabit myself
locked in carbon solitude?

I plunge my head under water,
glimpse an eel about my limbs, dangle my fingers in the murk,
feel barely-there jellies spiral in luminescence,
lilting fronds of weeds yoked to what always is,
bound shyly to edges of the dark.

I don't want to begin at the beginning,
sliding from amnion, thinness of eyelids not yet open,
translucent senses,
the first charge of air,
welcomed by receiving hands, safety assured.

Begotten

Badger skin hacked back by maggots
reveals a curd of bones,
heels, claws, tongue,
tacky like pitch.
I prop two flowers in its eyes,
death in the pines bent like and elbow,
the loam of life reduced to squirming decay.
An indigo beetle straddles the badger's flesh,
a crimp of legs
embedding in discharge.
I inhale the stench, surprised not to mind,
its jaws clenched,
teeth like darts,
gums misaligned.

I'll wear the same mask, corrode
in a mute husk, worms the filigree of my face.
I will endure,
unclench my hands,
while I lie, quite still,
tasting the blackberry wine of blood gone sour,
the bite of soil in my mouth,
sockets for light in the welts of my eyes.

I never knew the rigging
of my own taut sails.

The Moon Reveals Her Shadow

And I try to find mine.
How many people wear a disguise?
I can hold a fistful of fear but no more.
I can hold one lie —

I can't tell if I know how to see.
I empty my pockets. Feed the birds. Rinse out a cup,
smooth the bed.

It's dangerous not really knowing.
I have to come up for air.
A self-portrait doesn't paint the self,
only shows how one fits in the world,

wearing that wry smile:
a series of scribbles.

Advent

I went to close the curtains tonight but

dusk had not quite fallen. I didn't want

to miss the gentle slipper of night slope

across the dark. I waited to watch the sky

stain in hue, paused to glean opal shadows

pool in half-life under the moon. I die

a little, each day.

The Fish

He reels in a striped bass,
eyes, mica brimmed,
scales, thin,
like Etruscan coins.
He slits the carmine gills, carves
the bipartisan flesh from cavity walls.
Scallops hinge through eelgrass,
thousands of eyes, manganese blue,
shifting through the gargoyle of blood cloud.
The fish pounds, lips,
a molybdenum pout
smooth mouth-silk stained,
watercolour bleed.
He will part flesh
from its corset of bones,
discard the interlocking ether.
I could have saved it:
the argentium flowers
of its frayed skin,
a shimmering caul. Eyes, slag now,
bellows of lungs deflated,
senses cut,
my turning away, too shy
to ask of him, *please.*

Knot

'Ride into battle like a soldier,' the doctor said,

my legs spread,
womb-chalice emptied.
I never felt your birth water,

the blackberry knot of you
peeled away
from the direction of my heart;

his crisp white coat as sharp
as the scrape that blotted you out.

Intersection

What made her eyes milky?
Had she nursed a child?

Styrofoam cup in hand
bundled in a scarlet parka,
brake lights of passing cars blinking
in the dark,
she kept thanking me
and I kept telling her she was welcome,
handing her a hundred.

Live Haulage

The pigs will be slaughtered by now,
dragged by their tails
from the metal sidings of the lorry,
to wait on the dimly lit abattoir floor,
nostrils patiently inflating,
inhaling the fear of
death for a hog paid piecemeal,
speed of its killer inducing
inaccurate application of stunning tongs.
Pigs stuck from gullet to snout,
pink to red.
Pig holla.

Vole

Found concussed
at the edge of the road, I held you
like a pom-pom, your paws,
bony as an old woman's hands,

the dun of you,
marvelous in miniature.

    *

I will watch you die, mother,
the swell in your eyes
as the light floods in

like a freshly-washed sheet
flung across the bed.

Work
for Jake

Feel the full weight of the heart,
rowan red, irreducible
wrapped in membranes sheer enough
to detect lies, patiently waiting sod

field for plough.

MADE BY HAND

Dear Mr Ammons

I'm not in the habit
of writing to dead poets

>however I would like
>to write *you* a poem

for I too share your love
of cash register
>tape
>>the skinniness of the paper

a finely
sharpened pencil
uncurling the slightly soft
slightly unruly coil,
>how it spills from my desk
>in its own meanders

today   ice has formed
ampoules
at the edges of the lake
in some places even
like the shape
of sagging balloons

lugubrious clouds
I'm always looking inside cracks
trying to sift
out the gold

You write about the soul
describe it like a river
using
        prairie
        accretion
        poise

scum and foam

is this how the soul is?

why does home feel
        so far away?
        always
we want to walk home

I like the idea of having wings
I often dream of moths
        did you know the wingspan
of a silk moth
        is one hundred and fifty
        millimeters wide

and the micro moth
less than a mere tenth of an inch?

the soul weighs
just twenty on grams
maybe the same

    as the innocence
        we lose

private
peculiar
delicate

barely discernable

as the opening of the iris
      the very first time
the closing for the last
      and the in between.

Aurelia Aurata

Neither weight nor substance.
Imagine its beaching, sensory
hairs sloughed as it hits a tumbling of stones.
Once on shore its proteinaceous saline form starts to film,
a circular effacement, a halo on the sand.
Spy the lobed margins of its diaphanous bell, sewn
together with invisible ocean thread:
lappets, pouch, oral arms, it can detect
up from down seeking out the light, sensitive
to the sun's rainbow shaft.
Frilly arms comb the salty waters, muscles, delicately
pulsing, vacuum, hollow, no match for storms,
a moon jellyfish stranded
on the sand.

Wake

There is no reason why we can't learn to forgive.
It's only because we're afraid.
I watch you stir and I wonder,
shrieking in silence as roses on the wall hiss in my face.
The way you listen without ears.

I don't think it will be so hard to die.
All I ask is that you watch me.

There is no mercy when the eyes grow tired.
In shadow, twilight, stand like a burning mountain,
raw, vestigial,
time propitious, monoprint
of waking.

Roadkill

No one would think of the aftermath
or even notice
the blackbird lying sticky on the road,
flattened wings fanning their lineage
of bones like a fossil,
a pale green caterpillar in its beak, squeezed
our of grub skin,
fledglings left flustered in the nest.

I stop the car
to peel this unison of death
off the gritty tarmac
to place in the scrub.

To wonder, that all I have
is the idea of resurrection.
Suffering permeates
in a fine ether of sky,
blue, blue, sharpening my wits,

interrogation of crows,
scrappy in trees,
homing in for the pickings.

Filament

I pray for rain,
wanting angels
to hear me,
waterholes glazed   to crazy paving.

Where does prayer go;
grist of thought
released,
as strokes of breath
ascend?

No difference between
death and truth,
the microscopic element
of return.

Incessantly
scraping the earth with its foot,
an elephant insists on covering
                           a splayed skeleton,
light-years white.

Claiggan Bay, Islay
for Jake and Bess

One day you'll find the boxes
where I keep my favourite stones —
schorl, schist, obsidian,
in petal lined beds;
thistle-blue,
graptolites, tribolites,
ancient creatures pressed
in mountain slab.

The bay tallies its own hours.
Watch the graphite sheen
of pencil light on water.
Set your life to music.
Reset the dark stone.

Finding the Semibreve

Let's explore music
that takes us to the river
where her body reflects

sun and pink moon.
This is her swell.
Come hear the beautiful

bones of the white bark tree
leaning over the river,
the river's apostrophe.

Come take us down
to the shifting resound
of the levigated sand,

to the black beads
and dashes of spawning
toads. Come take us

down inside the river's
twisting frame, through
sunlight shafts, murk,

to the semibreve, flame.

Offering

I touch the tiny paws of a mole,
upturned in death, black fur
patinated like the slow pouring of oil,
pads, pink like a newborn, even fingernails.

A storm stirs, unpredictable,
the flow of solder,
washes you through, parts
the hairs on your underbelly, makes way
for maggots. They will writhe
on your un-marred body, velveteen
flesh, the eloquence of your limbs.

To keep digging, blind:
I want eyes for darkness.

Made by Hand

This is my undertaking:
to spoon myself to the deep,

enter within-ness,
my pelagic heart pierced, riveted

to what may always be broken,
the gravely slippage of stones,

a wren snagged by wind,
thrown to a casket of waves,
her erratic flight loaded with intention.

I slide my body under green water,
amidst the shift of sea shapes

into the permanence of particles sinking,
hermit crabs, origami of bones,
hatches closed.

I go to where there is no thought,
inside a Minotaur of silence.

Notes

The glade has razored sides
from the felling of the trees,
each crest fallen
as the chainsaw glides in swift arrest,
tears them belly to knees.

Cleaved. We gut her,
strim her,
scour her,
earth's deep ravines,
sluices for our overflow.

A wasp struggles, caught
in the tide's line, exoskeleton
and wings crisped by a layer
of crystalline salt. Unable to fly,
it burns. By degrees.

Germination

I said no to dissecting a frog,
cleaving a lobster in two,
disemboweling a pheasant, shot
feathers in a rosary
of fool's gold about its neck.
I said no.

I imagined chloroform whirring
undetected in the frog's lungs
paralysis locking its hind legs;
permanent bent forks.
Eye membranes would shut,
slathering it blind.

There is no majesty
in the severance of light.

To feel the space around
the human heart,
the unwind of its ribbon,
a black flowering germinate.

Prayer

No more
than a dandelion
releasing its parachute seeds
into violet air.
The channeled whelk
in its broad bodied whorl,
spire, sutures, aperture,
donning to the damp
edge of sand
its coin case capsules,
baby whelks, replicas
the size the heads
of sewing pins.
Newly-hatched
turtles in their leathery
scuttle. Moon for eyes.

Mordant

The peach tree in my garden

                                                                                            took

five years

to yield fruit —

polka dot blight,

                                                                                           amber

crusts

bored by wasps, fertile nap
of festering skins.

Now the architecture of its branches are laden
with mordant suns.

Overnight,

                                                          spiders have strung garlands

sewing up plants   into the early hours,

the patience

of a wasp,
ardently seeking   one sweet drop.

The naming of things:

                            wanting —

A coroner in his white coat

unable

      to detect how I'd stood there

tremulous   watching.

They'd never find the privacy of my yearning
in an autopsy.

Listen

Unhinged in their trenches,
seed skins break, sheath-splitting,
shoots searching for light,
radicles seeking black water,
pulling the ground. Each
seed, more than itself:
partisan, brethren,
refugee. Light coaxes. Ranks
of seedlings swim through
soil, reaching to shafts
of sun. Each plant transpires,
each stoma opening and closing,
the rush of simple sugars
passing through blade and stem.
All flesh is as grass.
The oat grass yields spiky
fruits with bearded awns,
as the barley and rye.

Seal

I came upon a seal, eyes gone first.
Gulls hammered a hole, sharing the same pierce,
entrails slathering sand.

That sound I can't hear is for my own protection.

I pry back the silky fur, inspect
the napthol-red wound, smell honey-sour,
drag the seal by its winged foot
to the edge of the sea,
the succumbing,
as the moon rises, hips up.

Tincture

The moon is like a bruise.
I crush petals,
release their sap,
rub the elixir into my fingers.
I can make fire, hover
like a dragonfly,
aurelion matrix of veins,
thorax like rust.
Pulse of the asp's belly,
cold heat of her satin scales,
cloaca opening in secret:
clove brown clones
obedient to slither and coil.
Make my pyre. Burn me
on burial water so
my sparks become stars.

Do I Qualify

As mad for carrying a magnifying glass in my pocket?

I stop to peer at a weed,
the rings that wrap a worm, vanes
of a wind-blown feather.

Do I qualify as vain
staring in the mirror,
looking into my eyes?
Blue irises change colour depending
on the weather.

Am I professional standing at the sink,
for years my back turned
so no one would see me cry?

Madness
is nothing more
than a perfection
of being
alone.

Words Like Skylarks

Indigo child
traverses fields, gathers long reeds of grass,
seed heads like data.
Collects bones,
sees inside white, only
wants the grave,
grave as sea,
as spume,
as rattlesnake.
Don't trade one eye for another.
Don't be casual.
Handle soil.
Remark on it.
It forgives nothing,
refuses nothing.

Finding Mu
Japanese word used in koans implying the absence of something

for Robert

I'd like to go out West.
See the colours:
madder lake, vermillion,
the pink of strawberry ice cream,
desert butterflies who love the cold,
the indigo light of darkness where Jupiter loops
her iced wings rimmed in an apothecary of blues.

Throw a stone into a river.
Here one has no name.

When the Soul Wakes

Child of the interior,
light more lavender
than light,
shifting inside illusions.

The always-smouldering sky,
madder and mauve.
I cannot fathom
how these colours were mixed
and let to drip and sink
so shadow-less,
reabsorbed by cold sand,
stored in the hole of a shell.

I sleep under a sky watching me,
its long eye roving,

that I may wake, infused
with intelligence,
a soul in its dark water.

I'm Not a Lover of Love Poems

Memory turns on a spit,
the shapeliness of smiles.
I cling to your bones –
clavicle.

Together, watching the river,
its oil,
at night.

You know how I am soothed by grey.
In the carbon paper dark,
the moon fills me with milk.

      *

I'm not a lover of love poems.
I wouldn't know how to write one.

I can't sit down.
The chair doesn't hold me.
I have to organize.

I spend my time,
an empty field.

These Are How Delicate?

The snail, writing life-lines
in slime, lustre of moonstone.

Meadows opening
and closing in shadows,

speech and its betrayal.

Trying to find the word
like the thin space between
dicotyledons.

Smudge of black ink on my fingers.

A flicker, face deep,
digging for ants in the grass.

*

I don't mind being lost,
standing in a wood,
for the trees see me.

I admire everything that falls.

Vitreous-orange-saffron-curl
of wind-snipped leaves from trees.
I am one, they many.

Tint of a dream,

Padparadscha sapphire hue.

Sun sliding down the mountain.
Violation of dying stars,

the order of which all
unfolds.

Room 6 1 2

You came to the hotel dressed
in a suit, just for fun.

I greeted you in black lace.
You proceeded to plait my hair.

We lay for a while, clammy
as stinking fish. We talked. Didn't touch.

It was all I could do to look at you.
We spread our supper on a towel,

finished it off with caramels and champagne.
Why such concern about sheets?

Room 6 1 2. Sounds like bruises. A ring
on the table that held a promise and a lie.

DRAWING WITH THE HEART'S LINE

Elemental

She walks out to the cave, knee deep in grass. A vermillion hum. Light dipped in sugar, an amoeba, a kaleidoscope, a book, a single filament of spider's silk, a lasso. With her hands she paints solely in green: a green eyelash, a green spoon, a green drum. Talks to trees, particularly one. Sticks things in holes. Sticks things in her eyes. Took a vow. Took off her dress. Learned to fire a .22.

Translation

Puce-shot morning, guarded
by seraphs with gold bones.
Earth-language in flowers, metals,

multicolour ash,
lush magma, blood,
sugar of frost.

Words form
like boiled sweets dissolving.
Vowels round out: electro-

plate, brilliance of river.
Constructing consonants,
drawing

with the heart's line,
the scope
between earth and stars.

Dorset/Peru, Vermont

I turned into a woman somewhere on Route 7,
driving a road as unforgiving as steel,
resolve and adjustment painted
                line-white.
Since light is so vast consider it.
Everyone will tell you what they think.

You could take the turning for Dorset/Peru,
a turning you didn't know existed.
No more witless hope, no more sleep from sleep.

I fornicate with words: receive, crow,
disseminate, apologise — succour, plump, rush —

rub my own breasts. The sky's so perfect.

Tape that to the map.

Dora
after a poem by Eugenio Montale

Watching the two of you,

how you move him,
as he watches you walk through the lemon grove

trailing your hands over the trunks of the trees, merging
with olive shadows, your hair, shiny black rope.
He says he loves you Dora because you penetrate
his loneliness.

Tell me, do you know he watches
as you lie in the grass fondling your breasts,
your hand rummaging beneath your skirt,
your eyes aligned with stars?

When he holds you like no other,
do you weep like a child, for the child,
for the woman learning the lover's lore?

The white ivory of you
and how the light fades.

How you move me Dora
as he watches you
move among
the lemon
trees.

Blue Milk
for Bess

I still wear stockings, palest-pink
and fairy wings dyed black.

When I was a child I wanted
to disappear,
wipe the moon
from my atmosphere.

We'll never meet again like this:

February 16, 1991.

The sun goes down,
stains the sky tobacco.
My waters break.
I howl. You cry. How strange,
the placenta, plump
bagpipe.
My breasts fill with hot milk,
                                              blue milk.

You anoint me.

   *

August 28, 2007.

The police advise me not to break a thing.
To leave within the hour.

Your father says I'm unfit to be a mother.

He's hidden you away.

I strip without shame, spread my limbs.
I've never begged until now.
Where are you?
He won't look at me
but tells.

I step inside.
I know which vessel to smash:
wafer thin, opaque, ancient,
the colour of moon.
Shards shimmer in the courtyard,
porcelain moths dying in the light.

My nakedness they use against me
in court:
'an embarrassment'.

You'll find a mother's heart can be broken,
and in many ways.

We tell stories,
stack them like wet sand.
Watch the sea break them.

My love is savage.

Infusion

Of mussel-blue
passing into the cerebellum.

The silent moult

of a shell hidden in parched grass,
indigo edges devoured.

Loneliness can be contained
only so long

before we grind out
the symptoms,
find each hue,

have no more need for eyelids.

Annunciation

Pushing back from the dock, we quit the harbour.
Gulls pillage crabs from tidal pools,
maroon water.

Oh God, can I put on the sky,
undressed as I am, unperfected?

Luminous isinglass of sea-water,
no different from the feel of my own
birth fluid,
how, with the task
of expulsion, in the vernix of my skin,
I slithered like a wet seal,
air rushing into my lungs as I hit
the edge of the world.
It slammed me open —

A humpback, stove bolts sensing,
rams sand eels into its baleen sieve,
dives beneath the surface,
a dome of black.

Blue

I'm giving back my name.

Stuff the screams in a sock.
Pick the eye out of a sockeye.

How thrilling to lie in the dark,
hear the candle burn down.

I've eaten wax too long.

My life fits inside a shoebox,
a pretty blue.

My mouth trembles.
Stupid.

I could be stamens,
fish scales or a single shiver,

a stiff tongue.

No one can make me burn.

Loon

Watch a loon, most ancient of birds, in milk-glass-blue light
spear the membrane of the sea, a film of water about its head,
gold leaf of waves as it extends itself into oblivion,
phthalo-green. The loon bows, a dark angel.

There's life within shadow, an unseen miracle,
iridescence inside a silent current, the icy field of the sea
carding the loon's plumules, onyx wings.

Inscription

Inside my ring you inscribed, "Isn't this wonderful?"

I lie in the bath like liquid in a spoon.
I'm tired of mending,
black stitches, a run of them.
I'll pack my belongings like eggs clutched
from a nest: my collection of handmade bowls,
stems of dried grass from a field the year fireflies gathered
in droves, wooden Japanese dolls,
the books.
I'll pack up memory of the dogwood, the symmetry
of its flowers, wafers of pink.
I'll want the Fifties' watercolour of a Highland road in its original
frame.

I want to swim naked in the lake at night
under serrated stars,
listen to owls pry open the dark.

How Long Have You Been Satisfied?

See,
there are all colours
                            in grey,

then there is form:

a mountain,

and light like slip
that folds over a shell,

rubs us away
                          even
the backbone.

Cave Valley, Zion

She gets up at night to watch the moon
to make certain there's always light,
hoarse from jabbering,
the oil cloth of a soiled tongue.

It's possible to be brave
and ordinary,
intoxicated by
grief. Over time
the face meets sorrow,
a dark blue mist.

The willow's nearly bare.
In the green sleeve of waking
leaves twirl;
delicately torn prayers.

The red rocks hoard rovings of moonlight.
She sees the radiance
inside red.

Life Cycle

I had daisies for eyes as a child,
my voice box filled with soft white flowers,
empty
as a carton,

glued together with spittle like the nest of a wasp.
I sweep woodlice clustered
in dusty corners, bristle of legs, links
of their bodies gone dry, rolled
into balls like shot.

In the watery colour of morning,
the world, freshly washed of scars,
lifts its throat.

The light can blind.

It's easier to seek shadows,
traverse the forest,
lean into silence.

Scuttle of the jewel beetle,
as I open the lid of my gullet,
gristle of hinges.
I have kept it in its box
too long, marvelous
antiquity of green.
Antennae searching, it drops onto the soil,
leaving me
an imprint or iridescence.

In deep firs, calling alarm,
a wood pigeon, her voice ignited.

Tumbleweed

I had a tendency to agree.
Thought this allotted me love.
I closed the curtains when her headaches came on,
sewed her gifts for Mother's Day, over the years
gave her an assortment of heart-shaped stones.
She still dons anger, a tumbleweed
that never stops.

She ransacked the myth
of *Mother and Child.*

They will pad her face, smooth
the creases of disdain, pink her cheeks,
place her in a coffin.
I will study her, veneer
of eyelids, the jellyfish sheen
of her skin.
I'll thank her.
I'll have to deal with her clothes.

Hers is the metaphor of rumpled paper.

Smell the word feral.

Asteroid 433
First discovered near-earth-asteroid named after the Greek god of love Eros

Perhaps it sparkles with mica, spessartine or gold?
Never been there until now.
Do we think about how watery we feel?
Be an animal. Purr,
bray, whinny, flutter — stampede.
Hold something precious in your hands. Feel its light, weight.
Blush at the mere thought: a gemmy blush,
a radical blush, a star-like blush. Warm yourself
with feathers from a dove like Eros laughing. Move
so lightly, how a cloud dissolves, how we unhinge.
Wrap a dream just barely, but wrap it well.
Promises are wispy, flimsy, except for one,
always coloured red.

Flutter

Thank god for the flutter of light.
For hot-pink.
For frogs, innuendos and their purple
beat.
For symbiosis, stasis,
for the first kiss.
For sand-dollar courage.
The word,   bliss.
Flinging open the door to the sea, listening
to her sweep.
My silk stockings you slipped to the floor.
For Giotto, who illumed cerulean blue
and a promise,
broken
like a battered door. Thank God
for nipples,
for parting, sorrow,
for rivers that wind, oxygen, beauty-sleep,
a risk,
for my first taste of death,
the taffeta of love.

THE CONSEQUENCES OF INTIMACY

1. **The Boyle's King**

I never liked the combination of black and white.

The king snake hangs round my neck,
still warm.

I'll slice its belly,
dig out its spine.

I don't have to be good.
Who watches anyway?

Am I a hussy?

I'll save the best of me for death.

Is it merely privacy we crave?

2. **Collide**

I swallowed his sperm from a teaspoon.
He said I turn his skin inside out.

Maggots roil beneath the snake's skin,
sequins of scales.

A smile sits inside my face
as his finger pillages the dark.

3. **Skin**

We dropped its bones in bleach,
strung them on marline.

I'm everything that can't be seen.

Make one demand.

Hear your heart,

every yearning compressed
in skin.

All That's Possible

Lies in the hands like curd.
Face incredible love.
Howl it.
      Mark it on the body.

Don't listen to any more impoverished poems.

Femur
to Rob

I bring home the bone.

   *

He was born breathing in.
I was born breathing out. He asked
what I wanted.
I wrote it on a piece of paper: lazalu.
He ate it.

He studied swallows, said they were God's needles.
Always drew angels.
Born, 1949. April.
He wrote on scraps. Declared he should have been
a fish.

He helped write this poem.
Call it his obituary.
We sat together eating langoustines.
Glencoe. June.

No one but a bad seed would draw
in Johnson's dictionary.
He agreed with Alice:
"What use is a book without pictures…"

He needed organizing,
knew I'd never been seen.

I slide his bone along the cool, white sheet.
It enters me like a fish,
breathing.

Renegade

Let go wanting acceptance.
Denude a fish of its scales.
Become the sweetmeat of the sea,
its concoction of forms,
the salience of an horizon,
isotope-blue.

Bird

I've been picking up roadkill since I was a child —
intrigued
amalgam of bone   skin   feathers   fur
fused to tarmac —
                      viscera
jewels,
the carnelian gleam,
emulsified eyes, bespoke
claws,
web of connections ground down

I can't leave it on the road,
a still-breathing gull,
puzzlement fixed
in the gaze,
the belligerence
of death fast approaching,
the lull —

sky pressed like clay,
submission,
holding the slur of a body,
soul
        thinning out.

Talking to Myself

We've done this before.
She says you're a song rising,
leaning into wind and celestial navigation.
And we must talk for *I* am busy picking out
the running stitch,

for there *are* such lovely circles and cross hatchings in water
and *he* says you must go inside and feel what bleeds
for it's raw and tender and I see it now. For it isn't ghost-
colour anymore.

Words of the Night-Time Angels

Walk awhile under
the Byzantine sky.
No abstractions here.
No philosophy.
It's impossible not to inhale
the fume of the night-blooming flowers,
each petal, dark-rimmed,
rinsed gold.
We'll talk with topaz tongues,
with wings unfurled like the sails
of a great ship nearing home.

Make a new vow.
Remember the impeccable colour
of twilight, the undying
quantity of blue and the moon
as she ascends.
Go to the sacred forest. Remove
your clothes. Allow the cambium of your body
to be cleansed. Cry out.
Jump.

GONE TO EARTH
To Rob

Black and Blue

I watch you slap your spatula feet along the sand.
Your eyes sing in that darkened ink spot, drawn around with yellow.

You pick through the curls of molluscs jig-sawed on the sand
and scratch your living in the shards.

Sometimes you find pearls protrude from oyster moire,
white bones and maybe a fishing line.

You often leave a feather or two stretched by the wind
like the tines of a fork. I pick them up and feel I know you.

Just a little. I run my fingers along the length of rib,
realigning the sliced spokes of these blades from your wings.

You persevere amidst the nubs of the sea,
gilded with coins of light, rolling loose like change.

I place myself on the sand, like a stone.
I imagine the weight of you were I to hold you in my hands.

Gull

The mound of earth is still humped
from the disturbance of my trowel.
You lie there cold in the ground.
I see your sepia eyes.

From the disturbance of my trowel,
the soil cleaved as I buried you down.
I still see your sepia eyes
as you are slumped, there in my hands.

The soil cleaved as I buried you down.
You'd been hit and left on the road.
As you slumped there in my hands,
I remember the weight of your breast.

You'd been hit and left on the road,
swirling with damaged wings.
I remember the weight of your breast
as you lifted your head to see mine.

Swirling with damaged wings
and tipping onto each side,
you lifted your head to see mine.
Then I scooped you off the road.

And tipping onto each side,
fear tight in the round of your eye,
I scooped you off the road,
feathers like flurrying snow.

Fear tight in the round of your eye,
scissored shapes of those broken wings,
so white like flurrying snow.

Scissored shapes of those broken wings,
no planing into the sun,
you were twisted and misaligned
and I held you in my arms.

No planing into the sun,
as the sun seeped in through the clouds,
and I held you in my arms
at 6 a.m. On the road.

As the sun seeped in through the clouds,
crumpling there in my palms,
at 6 a.m. On the road
I carried you into the scrub.

Crumpling there in my palms,
I felt the flower of your heart.
I carried you into the scrub
stroking your tabular wings.

I felt the flower of your heart
with the gliding of my hand,
stroking your tabular wings
as my face was seared by tears.

With the gliding of my hand
and breath, deep and full,
as my face was seared by tears
the heel of my boot came down hard.

With breath, deep and full,
crushing your ruby brain,
the heel of my boot came down hard,
crumbling your skull like a rose.

Crushing your ruby brain,
I took the glistening—from your eyes,
crumbling your skull like a rose
and smashing your lacey bones.

I took the glistening from your yeses,
gave you darkness of all night's dark.
Smashing your lacey bones,
you became the immortal bird.

Gave you darkness of all night's dark,
yet you rest now in the lightest light.
You became the immortal bird,
though you don't even have a name.

Yet you rest now in the lightest light,
placed in the deep of ground.
Though you don't even have a name,
your memory lies under the mound.

megapera novaeangliae, the big wings of the sea

so slowly came the boat to rattle
in the choppy seas
so that when his rhythm
from the underneath
lifts him from the iron blue
he takes his breath
and we wait for flukes
and fins and fan-like feet
making prints
in a lob-tailng sweep
parting the waves like spears,
hurling his skin
to smash down and roll
belly up
heart deep, the boom
slushing in his thick knotty veins
in beautiful fat,
whale,
and he kinks his swim
to head for the boat
and hangs his giant eye
and hairy beard
and scoops and sluices
the juicy sea
to sieve the krill
then comes to wait
at the hard metal hull
he watches
as we peer over the rail
cameras bobbing
flapping jackets

in the rain
he feasts
drawing in his bubble net
of minnows caught in millions
huddling in the gargantuan balls
his fringed baleen sieves
locking like dungeon doors.
And the froth of the sea dissolves his form
and he dives to the squid
and phosphorescence
and luminescence
down in the deep.
here his lungs slow,
holding him,
sustained.
then particles of spray
as his sudden breach
leaves salt whips
as he heaves
hurdling his heaviness
upwards to sky.
he plunges with hard breath
gashing the water's line
and his weight
suspends him as he swells with the sea.
nudging his fins
along the bow
we stare into each other's eyes
two breeds apart.
what is is that he holds
behind those globed eyes
in the rivers of his sea realm,
in his aqueous dream

as he slides through the sea
looking in my eyes
through and into me.
he turns,
slips quietly
then softly sails away
as I am standing
still,
in the rain.

An Autobiographical Sequence Poem
Taken from the Story of Thumbelina
For Bess

I.

Light Found in the Boom of Things.

Amidst the darkened sleeves of the lily pads, where the pike lopes in the half shade, where the wild willow weeps, where moon-milk nests in the shallows down on the big broad stream, in the brooding ink night and when dawn scuffs the sky, I wait for her to come and find me, stranded here, seated on the brim of a great green leaf, water all around me. Kindness is like down floating up-stream. Will she come and find me with her delicate thumbs? I sense her in the hinges of flowers. I see her in their tiny faces. I cannot look into snail's eyes nor into the hearts of eels. I cannot sense where my skin begins or where my skin ends. I feel the cold dark germination of pond weed. A tiny gauze of gloom. I cannot touch the sky nor reach the river-bank's flowers. They chaff as the wind moves in. I cry tears like drums into these ancient waters where all is remembered. I count the petals in a stone, waiting for butterflies' wings.

II.

Indigo Child.

I don't want there to always be change. Sign language can seem more beautiful than the words we speak and I have butterflies inside my head. She is a pretty bright thing. Frisks her wings at the edge of the teetering corn. She folds and refolds, the wind moving her buff body and lemon wings. In possibility. I would like to tie myself to her with the sash of my dress. And we would cross the mottled river all swish with ripples and weeds. She would lead me. I sometimes sway with a music that passes through me. And I swear I can hear the speaking voices of the trees. I still have a child's face inside me, these things that pass through when I feel as if I am in the clutches of an enormous bird.

III.

Self Portrait.

Butterflies are always beautiful. How they spread their boomerang wings. I like to watch leaves quiver. And the sun slant her violet shadows taking away the light from hidden away places. I look from upside down. Silvered vantage point. I talk to myself. Lyrically. Frayed. Outside the window is a cracked flower pot. I will fill it with little sharp stars. I walk along alleyways, plumes of dandelion seeds glittering air. I have left my belongings in the cold dark cellar of the earth. A blanket and a flower. I just came in from burying a bird. I saw my reflection in his coloured eye. Claws like forks spread to receive. Words fall off my tongue like sappy sweet plums and dust will collect where the paragraph ends.

www.ingramcontent.com/pod-product-compliance
Lightning Source LLC
LaVergne TN
LVHW051659080426
835511LV00017B/2635